The Korean War

Anyhow!

A decorated soldier
remembers a Forgotten War.

Mary

Thank you!

Don R. _____

Anyhow!

On The Front Cover

A silk portrait of Don Collen by a young Korean named Quak. "The kid took my two dollars for the portrait, then disappeared," Don says. "I was surprised he even came back."

On The Back Cover

Three commemorative battle coins, each representing one of the many battles Don Collen fought in.

Battle of Old Baldy – One the hilltop outposts, Hill 266, was nicknamed *Old Baldy* after repeated artillery fire had stripped away all of its top greenery. Old Baldy changed hands many times between the Chinese and United Nations' forces, but ended in the hands of the Chinese at the end of the war.

"About all I can say about Old Baldy is that it was much steeper than most and had more caves and places for the enemy to hide. My first sergeant got killed on Baldy. He was a close friend and had a family in the states. I had a rough time swallowing for quite awhile after that."

Battle of Pork Chop Hill – The hill was part of the United Nation's main line of resistance along the border between North and South Korea. After securing Old Baldy, the Chinese began nightly raids on Pork Chop Hill. After numerous short-term battles and a high number of casualties, U.N. defenses decided to abandon the hill.

"When I left Korea in November of 1952, the fighting was still very severe. We took it many times and vacated it many times – and lost many lives. It was truly a game of chess using military personnel as pawns merely for leverage in the oncoming treaty. That fact never set right with me."

Battle of Triangle Hill – Another strategic hill, Triangle Hill was less than 20 miles north of the 38th parallel. Like many hills during the war, possession changed hands often. After a lengthy and costly offensive, the fighting stopped with no appreciable land gained by either side.

"Like most battles, all hills received a number, such as Hill 106 or Hill 1109. This was mainly for calling in air or artillery support. Most hills (battles) included the following: take the hill; hold the hill; retreat from the hill – then do it again. Triangle Hill was no different. So many lives lost!"

Photo – Don and his father, Pop

Anyhow!

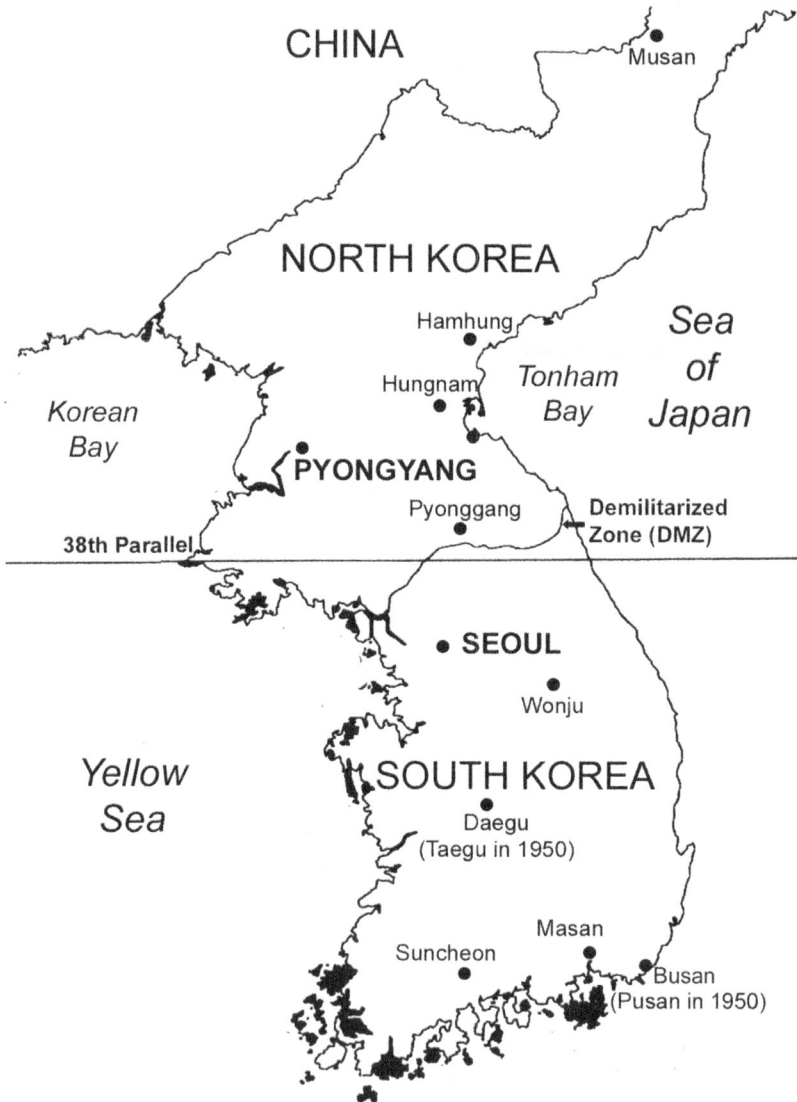

CHINA

Musan

NORTH KOREA

Hamhung

Sea of Japan

Hungnam

Tonham Bay

Korean Bay

PYONGYANG

Pyonggang

Demilitarized Zone (DMZ)

38th Parallel

SEOUL

Wonju

Yellow Sea

SOUTH KOREA

Daegu (Taegu in 1950)

Masan

Suncheon

Busan (Pusan in 1950)

The Korean War

Anyhow!

A decorated soldier
remembers a Forgotten War.

As told by
Don Ashton Collen

Recorded by
Peter Randolph Keim

KeimRanchBooks

Anyhow!

"My life and death recollections from the Korean War are based on factual events from my combat experiences. What I've written here is pure gospel." – Don Collen

Cover Graphics: P. Randolph Keim
Editor: Gini Holcomb

Printed in the United States of America.

For this, and novels by Peter Randolph Keim,
go to Amazon.com. You'll find classic westerns, detective
mysteries, children's stories, Christian/Spiritual novels and
epic Zombie stories.

Dedication

First, to my lovely granddaughter, Jenna Knutsen. When my wife died from breast cancer in 1996, Jenna – only ten years old at the time – came to my home and brought meaning to my dismal life. At that time she suggested I write about my life and my war experiences. I am following through with her request. Thank you, Jenna.

Second, to the over 36,500 G.I.'s (Government Issue) who didn't come back. Also, to the nearly 100,000 severely wounded who did come back. I saw so many of them die in action. I truly thank them for the gift of freedom that they died for. One of those brave soldiers was Pee Wee Young, who got to Korea before me, but whose soul is still there. Pee Wee was a very good friend of mine during high school. Thank you, Pee Wee.

Anyhow!

A brief note from
Peter Randolph Keim

As World War II came to an end, the Japanese Empire was the topic of world-wide discussion. Part of that talk was an imperial colony, Korea. In 1943, it was decided that the United States would occupy South Korea, and the Soviet Union would occupy the North. It was determined that the 38th parallel would be the dividing line for the temporary occupation, which began in 1945.

Negotiations for a unified country lasted into 1949, when the United States and the Soviet Union withdrew their forces from the region. However, skirmishes between the north and south continued along the 38th parallel. On June 25, 1950, 75,000 well-trained and well-supplied North Korean soldiers, invaded the south. Two days later, the United Nations Security Council sent forces to help defend the south.

The United States committed the majority of forces and led the operation. A small United States task force left Japan to hold back the north's relentless march until a much larger Allied force could be assembled to assist. By the time the north and south converged on Pusan, U.N. defenses were fully operational. On September 16, U.N. forces began pushing the north back to the 38th parallel. The tide had shifted, and the U.S.-backed forces now sought to liberate the entire peninsula by defeating the north.

China had different ideas.

Threatened by the U.N.'s push into North Korea, China warned they would consider it an armed aggression against Chinese territory. When the U.N. forces continued north, on October 25, the Chinese sent troops into the north. The fighting along the 38th parallel had started once again.

An armistice was signed on July 27, 1953. Korea was divided along the 38th parallel, called the Korean Demilitarized Zone. Estimates of lost lives, military and civilian, exceeded 5 million. The Korean War was called *The Forgotten War* because of little public attention from a war-weary world, but the soldiers who fought, and families who lost family members, will never forget it.

One such soldier is Don Ashton Collen.

A very brief note
from Don Ashton Collen

At first, I wanted to write this in answer to my granddaughter's request about the Korean War, but there's more to me than just my time in Korea.

Pop and Mom
This is *not* fiction.

My father – hereafter called Pop, was born in Houtsdale, Pennsylvania, on September 2, 1882. My mother – hereafter called Mom – was born in Jackson City, Ohio, on March 11, 1881. They were married in Welston, Ohio, on June 8, 1904. Pop started working in the coal mines when he was just 15 years old. Both their parents came from Germoe, England, roughly a five-hour drive southwest of London.

After their marriage, Pop and Mom lived in Welston, where Pop got a job with Lehigh Portland Cement Company. Before you could blink, they started having children. Later they moved to Mason City, Iowa, where Pop got the position of assistant engineer at the Lehigh cement plant.

And they had more children.

Pop remained with Lehigh Cement Company until he was forced to retire at just 65 years of age. While Pop was busy at his job, Mom was the very definition of a housewife. She had even more children – 15 in all – which gave her no option but to stay home and raise them the best she could. While Mom was a calming presence in the house, Pop was a militant type, but a good man. He was always a comedian and a great philosopher.

During the Great Depression, a lot of his workers at the Lehigh plant had to be laid off. They would come see Pop for help, and he would always give each of them a $20 bill. Back then, that was like half of Fort Knox in today's dollars. Those good folks would always say thank you. Five years later, they got their jobs back, and they would bring big baskets of fruit to thank Pop – very tasty!

Anyhow, one day one of the workers asked Pop why he had so many kids.

"Guess I just went to bed with my engine running," Pop would say.

Next question would be why did he stop having kids?

"Hell, I didn't stop!" He'd laugh. "She just ran out of eggs."

Mom was 43 years old when I was born – one last egg.

On the philosopher side, Pop had lots of sayings he'd share with us kids. To me, when I was young, I had my favorite.

"Know a little bit about a lot of things," he'd say. "and not a lot about one thing, and you'll always have a job." How right he was.

I've been a machinist, an auto mechanic, a marine mechanic, a surveyor, a graduate Forester with a Wood Technology Specialty, a chemist, a log buyer, a logger, and Lord knows what else. Whenever I was out of work at one profession, I always got a job at one of the others – thanks, Pop.

Mom, on the other hand, was a perfect mother – nothing like the *working* mothers of today. Mom was available twenty-four hours a day for Pop and all us kids. Why shoot! Mom and Pop were parents to all us kids and the entire neighborhood.

Anyhow!

Pop's Fairness

One thing I gotta touch on was Pop's fairness.

To be honest, I guess I never really understood it. He would always take time to explain his actions, especially after he dished out one of his good whippin's with a leather razor strap. Oh, that dang strap! Whippin's were always in the bathroom with the door closed and our pants and shorts huggin' our ankles with our hands on our knees. Oh, how we wanted to rub our stinging butts, but Pop made us hold our position while he sat on the toilet seat – then came the lesson.

"Do you know what you did to get this punishment?" He would ask, and I'm quotin' here.

When I think back, we better have had a good correct answer, or he would add one more swat to the next punishment. I think Pop had part elephant in him, 'cause he never forgot – what a memory.

The family was very close. Like most families, we had inter-family arguments, but nothing serious. (But let someone outside the family create a problem, and God help them.) The system was simple. Mom would write down what happened and who did it, and when Pop would come home, he would do the punishing. One, two, or three razor strappings on your bare butt. Talking back to Mom was an automatic three strappings that would take place. Lord, that did hurt, but seldom did that act get repeated. Pop's strappings were usually justified, but his fairness was a lesson in itself.

Anyhow, back to Pop's fairness. The neighborhood kids always played a game called *bounce out* in the street in front of our house. If you caught the ball on the first bounce, you moved up one position. When you caught it on the fly, you changed positions with the player. A fun game when there's no television, internet or iPhone. Anyhow, here's the story.

One time the batter hit it so hard, it went about 300 feet before rolling to a stop in the curb gutter. No one felt like going after it. Me, being the youngest at about 7 years old, finally got designated to go after it. Lo and behold, under that ball was a one dollar silver certificate. I grabbed the ball and the dollar and went running back to show Pop what I found – dumb! I threw the ball to the players and went out back to the garage to show Pop the dollar.

"Did you steal it?" Was always the first thing he'd say. After explaining how I found it, he sat me down on the bench and started explaining something to me.

"If the batter hadn't hit the ball so hard, you would not have found it. Right?"

"But, Pop . . ."

"And if that pitcher hadn't pitched it right, the batter couldn't have hit it that far. Right?"

"But, Pop . . ."

"And if none of the fielders could catch the ball, it went on its merry way to where you found it. Right?"

"But Pop, but Pop . . ."

By this time I felt lucky if I got a penny. To make a long story shorter, all the kids got a nickel each, and I ended up with a dime. Believe me, I knew better than to say, "But Pop," ever again. His last statement was, "Do you agree?" I almost bit my tongue off. That's the type of fairness my Pop had. I took my dime and ran to the store with it.

As for me,
Don Ashton Collen

I was born October 1, 1929, into this family of 14 children and two amazing parents – George W. "Pop" Collen and Grace "Mom" Turner-Collen. My birth made it 15 kids and two parents. All lived good lives except Clifton, who died of "cyanosis" (blue baby) at 6 months. He was born December 23, 1920, and at the time there was no medical knowledge for the cure (operation) to correct that problem.

Now, I'm the only one still alive.

Anyhow, my schooling was Monroe Elementary for 5 years; McKinley for one year; Monroe Jr. High School for 3 years; Mason City High School for 3 years; Mason City Jr. College for 2 years; and 4 years at Iowa State College. Two years in Korea.

My primary outlook during those younger years was based on hunting, fishing and camping, etc. I became quite an expert with a rifle, handgun and shotgun. Very useful when I was in Korea.

My allowance was a nickel a week. Those Liberty V or Buffalo Head nickels were usually spent on fuel for the Model A Ford. My sister was taking us and neighbor kids to a hunting or fishing spot, then picking us up at a certain time. Man, did we get in a lot of trouble. But it was all kid stuff, nothing malicious. And believe me, we paid in many ways for what we did. My youth (until I went to war) was great. I had little to complain about.

I remember the kinds of trouble we got into as kids. One night, we were trying to help this farmer get rid of skunks because they were killing his chickens. In Iowa, we had a lot of skunks, and they weren't all politicians.

Anyhow, this one night we shot and killed two skunks for this farmer, and he made us take and bury them for him. That way we got to hunt pheasants on his farm. In burying the skunks, we had to handle them – *very carefully!* The smell permeates the air around them, so naturally we smelled like skunk. Everything around us smelled like skunk, so we got used to the smell. About 9pm, I had to get home, and when I walked in like nothing happened, the family vacated the house, and I got chewed out by my mom. The end of the skunk story is I had to take a bath in mashed tomatoes with all my clothes on. I found out the other guy had to do the same thing. It must cancel out the odor as I was in that bath mess for over an hour. That was the end of our skunk hunting.

Then there was the time we went crawdad fishing, both for bait and to eat. Believe me, they're good! We chipped in gas money, and my sister took us out to a little creek north of town. She dropped us off and said she would be back at 8pm to pick us up – in Summer it was light til 10pm. One of our friends came by and talked us all into going out on the Winnebago River to catch carp. He had a car, and it was only 2 miles away. Carp are not much for taste, but they are great sport, about 20 to 30 pounds on a fly rod. What a fight! Well, needless to say – hey, we were only 12 or thirteen years old – we got so wrapped up fishing, we forgot about my sister Dixie picking us up two miles away. It was 9pm and starting to get dark. We had no ride to get home and the nearest road was a quarter mile away.

Anyhow!

Anyhow, we ran to the nearest road, and luckily my buddy Bob's dad was coming home from work. It was still light enough for him to see us on the roadside, so he gave us a ride home. Bob lived right next door to me. I walked into my house not knowing the whole neighborhood was looking for us.

My sister chewed me out.

My brother beat the pulp out of me.

The whole neighborhood hated me for at least two weeks.

"Wait until Pop gets home," Mom said.

"Ulp!"

True to Mom's word, when Pop got off work at 6pm, he was waiting for me with his razor strap. I didn't get much sleep that night mainly thinking about that razor strap. However, it wasn't the last of my numerous *stunts*.

When I was in Jr. High, High School, and Jr. College, the friends I ran around with always went around looking for fights – 180 degrees from my parents' nature. I found dialogue much better than the bruises and blood I shed just for being dumb and stupid while in the growing years. We had a favorite place in a tavern in Manly, Iowa. It was on old Highway 65, ten miles north of Mason City.

In the 9th grade through Jr. College, I was fairly well built physically, 6' 2" and 185 pounds. I had broad shoulders, quite muscular, but no brains. When we were at the tavern, we would pick out a group of guys that had the same number in the group as us (usually four), and one of us would go over and insult one of them on purpose. Then came the fight and usually the bartender made us go outside. Back in the 40's, it wasn't hard to get a beer at an out of the way tavern. Needless to say, there was never any winners in a fight – just a bunch of losers.

Anyhow!

Anyhow, this one time we really were drunk, and we broke a lot of beer glasses by stacking them up. The bartender was busy, so we sent one of us up to always get more beer. I guess pitchers of beer was unheard of at that time. Anyhow, the glasses fell to the floor, breaking all over the place. We were beating on the bartender when about 12 guys in the tavern came over and beat the crap out of us before they threw us out. My friend Pete decided to drive, saying he was the most sober. Actually, he was the drunkest. We took the back roads so we wouldn't get caught driving drunk, and all four of us were minors, according to the law. The roads we were on were icy, approximately 1-2 inches thick with little rocks sticking up. All three of us kept telling Pete to slow down, but he just kept going fast.

Finally, Pete lost control, and we came to a halt at a 45 degree angle over a ditch that dropped 12 feet down - that was the bad part. The good part was we stopped about twelve feet from a concrete bridge rail. If we had hit that at that angle at least one of us would have been beheaded. There was a moment of silence, then one of my friends,Tux (his nickname because he was always so well dressed) sitting on my right hand side, spoke up.

"I'm getting out of here!" He said, flipping the door lever. He dropped out the door like a bullet from a gun.

"Aaaaahhh!"

After two seconds of dead silence. we heard a loud *thud* at the bottom of the ditch. I could see him on the ice in the ditch below because there was a full moon. I asked him if he was all right. In the gloom below he looked up.

"Yeah, but watch out for that first step," Tux laughed. "It's a son of a bitch!"

We walked the rest of the way home all bruised and battered – mostly from the tavern guys beating on us. I

Anyhow!

really don't know how my parents survived me. I guess God was saving me for the Korean War.

Anyhow!

Preparing
for War

My youth went fast – way too fast – and the next thing I knew I was at Fort Benning, Georgia, learning how to shoot to kill a person rather than a deer. It really comes as a shock. My military training was short-lived due to the Korean War, that really wasn't a war, so they called it a Police Action. It was escalating very rapidly. We spent mornings opening camps that had been shut down after the World War II era. Afternoons and nights were for combat training, etc. Not much time for sleep.

As I stated before, our basic training was cut short to about 4 or 5 weeks at Fort Benning. This was due to the fact that all the older WWII camps had been abandoned, and were in need of severe repair. This included Camp Gordon near Atlanta, Georgia. We were assigned to get that camp in readiness form as the Korean War was rapidly escalating, and they needed more G.I.'s getting into combat. We'd get up really early, around 4AM, and repair until mid afternoon. Then, we'd head back to Fort Benning for close combat, bayonet training, ducking live fire, and all other kinds of training.

I remember us on the Firearm Familiarization Course. The sergeant was in the pit with a guy from Arkansas who knew absolutely nothing about firearms. We were in a *column of ducks,* which is the next in line about 10 feet directly behind the pit. The sergeant was trying to identify parts of the rifle to the Arkansas G.I. and was not doing very well at it. He had just put a single round into the rifle and someone yelled something loud behind me. The startled G.I. in the pit wheeled around and the M-1 went off. The round went through the left thigh of the first G.I., then went through the lower left side of the body of a second G.I. After ricocheting off a 16x16 support beam, it went off buzzing into space. Both G.I.'s lived and immediately the G.I. in the pit disappeared. I never saw him or that sergeant again.

No surprise there.

Anyhow, one day at Camp Gordon, our platoon was to stay overnight for a massive guard duty. There was a large amount of 2-½ ton trucks loaded with various sizes of live ammunition. We were coming in and staying overnight so we could pull guard duty for them. We were issued our guard posts and given live ammo for our weapons.

To paint the picture further, it started to rain, and I mean big-ass rain and lots of it. I never saw anything like it. My guard post was about 300 feet long. I had to march back and forth between the guards at each end of that stretch. The checkpoint password at one end was "Cherry". The other end was "Potato".

Near the end of that four-hour duty, I must a have had most of Georgia's red clay packed onto my boots – damn heavy. I thought I was entitled to a half-minute break, so I sat down on the front bumper of a 2-½ ton truck. I couldn't have been there five whole seconds when I heard the *slosh, slosh, slosh,* of someone coming. I jumped up from that comfortable bumper and yelled.

"Halt! Password!"

"It's me!"

I knew my duty as well as the next soldier. "Password or I fire!"

Anyhow!

I could not see him because of the darkness and the down pouring rain. But somewhere out in the gloom I heard a voice speak up.

"Cherry and Potato."

I lowered my carbine and warned him. "Sir, you have to be more careful. The hair is still standing up on the back of my neck. I sure as hell could a shot you dead."

Anyhow, he sat down with me on the truck's bumper and had a cigarette. He told me I was doing a good job and said he had to go back and change his pants after that ordeal. He wandered off into the dark.

Sure made me chuckle.

The Army did give us a 30-day furlough prior to going to war. That 30 days went by so fast. The next thing I knew I was boarding a train in Mason City heading west. That was the only time I saw my parents cry.

"I'm coming back alive!" Was the last thing I said to them.

Anyhow!

Korea Bound

The railroad people were good people to me, just like most of the others we came across. I remember in Omaha, Nebraska, that I had to wait all night for the next train. There was no place to sleep, so I curled up on a bench in the washroom at the train depot. There were a lot of homeless hobos in there with me. In the middle of the night a cop came in and booted them out. I started to leave, and he held up a hand to stop me.

"Not you, Son," he said. "Go back to sleep and good luck."

It almost gave me a feeling of importance until I remembered where I was going.

It seemed too soon to arrive at Camp Stoneman, in Oakland, California. Then I found out I was considered *overload* for the ship that was leaving. They always have about 100 G.I.'s ready to board if the scheduled G.I. breaks a bone or gets sick or something. That way they can have a body ready to take their place and board ship without any complications.

Now, I had to wait a week until the next troop ship came in. Both good that I was still in the states, and bad because I had nothing to do. Luckily, a friend of mine was at Fort Berry in the Air Force. He was a Master Sergeant and knew my C.O., Lieutenant Lickteig. The last word I had had with my friend was from Omaha, Nebraska en route. He talked my C.O. into giving me a 4-day pass, and it would be

George's (my friend) responsibility to get me back on time to be on the next troop ship. George and I went north along the west coast all the way to Long Beach, Washington. We stopped at every place we could to cast a line for fish. George had the gear and at the time my enlistment papers acted as a fishing license. We had a ball, and he returned me on time.

We boarded the Lt. Bedouin two days later – about 2,500 capacity. We were on our way. Before I got on the ship, I made a vow that if I came back, I would move to Oregon or Washington after college.

Our first stop was Hawaii for fuel and maintenance. They gave us an eight-hour shore leave. Nobody had any money of any amount, so it was just a lot of walking around.

Eight hours later we were on our way again. About halfway to Japan, a Puerto Rican soldier got acute appendicitis. I got to watch a transfer of medical personnel at sea from a troop ship – we had no doctor – to a top line destroyer. Thank God for calm seas. Then we got on our way to Japan. A few days later, we arrived at Osaka, Japan. On the way over, it was kind of weird. Very low morale and the majority thought they would not be coming back – and a lot of them didn't. It was a necessary war against communism, but a very strange war.

Anyhow, at Osaka, we got our shots, and all of us got a new MOS (Modus Operandi Status, Latin for a method of operation) – Combat Infantry. I was reassigned from Artillery to Infantry. Not good! I felt like they were painting a target on me for the North Koreans and Chinese to shoot at. We did get a week's reprieve to let the medical shots wear off.

We finally boarded the troop ship and shipped off to Korea. The only port open and friendly was Pusan. The

North Koreans and Chinese had advanced south to form the Pusan Perimeter.

Luckily, the 7th Division and the 1st Marines had landed at Inchon. With that and our strength on the Perimeter, the North Koreans and Chinese were retreating rapidly to the north. They were afraid of getting trapped by the 24th, 25th, and 1st cavalry divisions from the Perimeter and the rapidly moving 7th and 1st Marine divisions advancing across the country west to east.

The first resistance of any amount was at Taegu. The Chinese had left a fairly large body behind to protect the retreat of their substantial army. My company's 250 men and five half-tracks were formidable. Each half track had quad fifty's on them and were chewing the Chinese and North Koreans with those 50's. The Koreans would *hiss* at them because they knew the killing power in them. When all were firing, it sounded like an irregular, loud *pok-pok-pok*. It was a continuous sound and very impressive.

SEOUL

Wonju

SOUTH KOREA

Daegu
(Taegu in 1950)

Masan

Suncheon

Busan
(Pusan in 1950)

Taegu

While on patrol during a brief lull in the fighting, I went upstairs into a shot up, bombed out schoolhouse to check if we had any unwanted North Koreans in there with us. There were none, but on a broken mirror there was the following statement:

My Creed
I do not wish to be a common man. It is my right to be an uncommon if I can. I seek opportunity – not security. I do not wish to be a kept citizen, humbled and dulled by having the state look after me. I want to take the calculated risk; to dream and to build; to fail and succeed. I refuse to barter incentive for a dole. I prefer the challenges of life to the guaranteed existence; the thrill of fulfillment to the still calm of utopia. I will not trade freedom for beneficence, not my dignity for a handout. I will never cower before any master nor bend to any threat. It is my heritage to stand erect, proud, and unafraid; to think and get for myself; to enjoy the benefit of my creation and to face the world boldly and say, this I have done.
All this is what it means to be an American.

By: Dean Alfange

Anyhow!

In Taegu was my first battle – my feet and hands. It was so very cold and wet, all my limbs were suffering. Many times my feet were so numb that I didn't know they were there. At times, I truly wished I was dead. It wasn't long before I found that the summers were almost as bad with intense heat.

Taegu was a real problem, because it didn't matter if the weather was icy colt or damn hot, you could still count on hearing the hissing of bullets all around you. One of the guys said not to worry. The ones you could hear missed you, but if you felt pain, it wounded you.

Nice to know.

Guerrilla Attack

One night in early 1951, we were moving up north just north of Taegu. It was heavy rain most of the time, but a rain/snow mix at other times along with strong winds as cold as ice. In the extreme darkness, my platoon got separated from the Company.

"Let's bed down and wait for daylight," our lieutenant said. "Stay within whispering distance."

We had a password, *MOTEL*, given to us that morning. Seemed quite appropriate considering the horrible weather, 30 degrees and heavy winds. I'd a given $500 for a warm motel room out there – oh, well!

Me and another guy fell into a natural trench and tried to stay warm. We nodded off into a *close* sleep, meaning we slept real *close* to each other to keep warm. About 1AM the whole area became full moonlight, bright with flares. Then we heard machine guns and rifle fire.

"Geez! Don't they know it's us?" My partner said.

"Those guys are not on our side," I told him. "Those guys are Chinese guerrillas."

He was newer than me and started firing back at them. I just about lost my lunch. I started hitting him over his helmet with my helmet.

"What the hell are you doing?" He yelled over the gunfire.

"I want to go home alive with my body intact," I answered

"What the hell does that have to do with smashing me over the head?"

I pointed ahead of us. "Do you see all those orange flames out there?"

"Yeah."

"Behind each of those flames is a guy aiming at your orange flame every time you fire your rifle," I said. "If you keep giving them an easy target, you can bet your name's on one of their bullets. Now, stop shooting and get down low and very friendly with the dirt!"

Anyhow, the next morning he said he was sorry. Luckily there were no injuries or deaths. A little later we found the rest of our Company. We continued northerly through Kwangju and Puncheon Pyongyang. The process was slow, as we would take a hill five or six times. Retreating each time by orders. Always losing men – many G.I.'s.

Korean Humor

You know when you see a movie about combat, there is a lot of humor, even some laughter between battles. The G.I.'s, like John Wayne or Robert Mitchum, would sit around sweating and smoking. They'd laugh at jokes and play fast-ones on their buddies. Sometimes there would be beautiful woman being a nurse or some such. The soldiers would flirt with her, make fools of themselves for her attention.

Well, in Korea there was no laughter and very few smiles. Most of the time you were just worried about going home in one piece. You tried to make a little humor whenever you could.

One day, it was my turn to go down to a small creek and fill the canteens. I grabbed 12 canteens and made sure they wouldn't rattle while I walked so, I didn't make an easy target for the enemy. I always checked for my tablets to chlorinate (purify) the water.

Anyhow, I crept down to the creek and started emptying what little water was left over in the canteens. While I was doing this, I looked up and there was a *papasan* (the head honcho, patriarch, of the family) peeing in the creek – upstream from me. I couldn't quite stand drinking his pee, even though I was going to purify the water with the chlorine tablets. I don't know if any of my buddies did this, but I emptied all the remaining canteens that had water in them into my own personal canteen until it was full. Then, just to be extra safe, I put two pills in it and shook it hard til I was sure the pills had dissolved. Then, I filled all the other canteens with stream water – and old papasan's pee. I put pills in each one and shook them good before taking them back to my squad. I didn't say anything, but I sure hoped no one got sick.

I wondered how many times someone did that to me.

Anyhow, all water sources in Korea were highly contaminated. We had to be very careful. For a short moment, I had a sneaky smile on my face as I returned the canteens to the men. What's that old saying, "What goes around, comes around".

Later that same day, we learned that we were nothing more than expendable pawns. The Chinese were playing the same game. Both sides merely showing their power to gain better treaty rights. It's rather tough to see yesterday's friend get half his head blown off. You kept thinking, *why him and not me?* Or *when is it my turn?*

No humor in that.

The Hard Part

Often times, when moving from one place to another, we would pass a Red Cross or Salvation Army stand. The Red Cross usually had coffee and doughnuts, but there was no excuse for what they handed out. I think the doughnuts were to throw at the Chinese! It surely would have meant instant death for them as hard as those doughnuts were. I have little regard for the Red Cross.

But the Salvation Army was another story.

The Salvation Army people were congenial and had soft doughnuts and good coffee. And they did not charge us 35 cents for them like the Red Cross did. They also gave us a small, 3" x 5" copy of the Old Testament and one of the New Testament. I read both copies thoroughly.

I never realized how brutal the Old Testament was. I guess they had a Korean War, too.

The only good thing is you forget about the cold and the wet and snow you lived in during the Fall, Winter and Spring. Then there were the extremely hot summers. Sometimes over 100 degrees.

I'm sure actual battle affects all combatants differently. I know it affected me a lot. All the time going to a definite and different battle area – it sure put fear beyond belief in my entire body and mind. I couldn't tell whether it was the thought of dying, the miserable weather, or just being a coward, but one of them made my teeth chatter. Possibly just the weather, but I do know it was fear.

Anyhow!

Then came the actual battle.

No longer was the fear there, because you knew there was a job to do, no matter whether you live or die.

No longer was there any hesitation, you just waded into it.

No longer did the *pizzzzt* of a bullet singing past your head, or a land mine going off, disrupt your focus.

No longer were you affected by the earth-rattling roar of an artillery shell going off near you.

With me, and it was sort of strange, all I could think of was the loss of freedom we'd experience if we lost. Going back to a free country – that's what mattered. The job had to be done!

No longer did you feel the nicks and cuts of the rocks and brush picking at you while you climbed up yet another hill. Sure, you kept your head down, but the fear was no longer there. You did silly and crazy things that could cost you your life, but you just did them. Always afterward, the fear welled up just before the vomiting, and you promised yourself you wouldn't climb another hill – but you do.

The worst part was that these sights and happenings live with you in nightmares for decades after you come home. You fight the same battles over and over. You see your buddies die, and sometimes you wish it could have been you who died instead.

Burial Detail

I am dead serious when I say this may be the last paragraph I write. No matter where it's located in the story, I hesitate in writing and entering it in my memories of the Korean War.

But this is part of war – the really ugly part – but a part, nonetheless.

It was a very hot day, and we were moving northeast up above the 38th parallel and just above the town of Pyongyang. We were in the normal *Route Step* move. That's a single file column on both sides of the road so vehicle traffic could use the road. Our destination was the harbor of Wonsan.

The next thing I know, a major came up beside me, grabbed my arm and told me and three others to follow him. Knowing the military, you never willingly volunteer for anything, but this was an order.

"Sir, I have to tell my lieutenant before I can leave," I said, hoping to get out of the duty.

"It's already been taken care of," he said. "Follow me!"

Knowing better than to argue with a major, the four of us followed the major to a Jeep and took off – where we were going we didn't know. We stopped beside four or five 2 ½-ton trucks with tarps halfway down. The smell was terrible. There was a cat digging a trench nearby.

The major said the trucks were loaded with a platoon of dead G.I.'s – part of the 24th Division. They had been mutilated to death, so we were told to be prepared when they pulled the tarp off the dead. We were given orders to make sure to remove one dog tag and jam the other between the front teeth and close the jaw as tight as possible.

I can still see their eyes.

They had been tortured while alive. They had some bamboo spikes holding their eyelids open. Bamboo splinters had been driven up under their fingernails to the first and second joints. Some had split bamboo tied to loose belly skin and rolled up to their chest. God only knows how and what other tortures were done. Some had been scalped. The worst was the horrific smell of their rotting bodies. I would think later that I could not do that to my worst enemy.

I'll never forget that.

Our orders were to carry the bodies to the trench and gently lay them down. We were also to check their pockets for any letters or identification. I believe I puked four times at the first body. It was the dry heaves from then on. I felt really bad at first, but then I saw the other guys doing the same.

I couldn't sleep good for over a week. Nightmares were common, and the eyes of the dead are always staring at me.

The farthest north I got was with the 24th Division at Hamhung. Many lives were lost for no reason. At least that's what I thought at the time. Often times the wind would blow the snow sideways with subzero temperatures. I was afraid to try to figure out the wind chill factors. We wore everything we had and would wrap our boots with clothing from the dead.

There were caves everywhere – the Chinese hid in them for safety and to attack us. Often you could hear our G.I.'s being tortured in those caves. As bad as it sounds, our enjoyment was watching the Chinese come out of those damn cave-like shelters on fire from the napalm our beautiful Air Force dropped – both Navy and Army.

The Chinese were great at psychological warfare. They would play records over loud speakers about going home – or actually being home. Then they would give the names of dead G.I.'s. They had ripped the dog tags off the dead and named them over the speakers.

Holidays were the worst for me. Seems like they loved to play the song, *I'll Walk Alone*. The reason I disliked it was it was my girlfriend Lael's and my favorite song back in the states. I would cry when I heard it.

I got wounded a of couple times, nothing serious. They would fly us back to a MASH Unit; they would patch us up; and then you we'd be back with our outfit a week later. We did some really stupid things when we were cold, wet and shaking like a leaf in a wind storm. I really think that's what makes a hero. I sure did some stupid things.

The hills and mountains all had numbers or nicknames. Like Hill 1109 or Hill 1080. The nicknames were Old Baldy, Pork Chop Hill and Heartbreak Ridge, etc. I think the numbers had something to do with elevation. I really don't know, but I climbed a few of them. All of them were pocketed with small caves or hollow spots. The Navy Aircraft Carriers and the Korean-based Air Force didn't care. They bombed, rocketed, and burned all of them along with the Chinese troops. Without the air power we had, our mortality rate would have been in the hundreds of thousands rather than the 36,500 we actually lost. I really think that sometimes in war, death is a blessing.

I remained in Korea for my R&R. If you stayed in the Battle Zone, it counted for when you could go home. For my week, I was assigned to the motor pool at the UNCACK base – United Nations Civil Assistance Command Korea. One thing you didn't do was leave anything loose, like something spare, or it was stolen.

Anyhow, one night my Korean Interpreter and me went out in a jeep with an extra tire for a 2 ½-ton troop truck. The trip took us up to Taegu. We changed the tire on the truck and left to come back to base. About halfway back, I saw a bright glow ahead of us. I told the interpreter to get the rifle out and have it ready. There was a lot of guerrilla action in the whole area. We came upon a 2 ½-ton U.N. truck burning and quite heavily damaged. The G.I. driver was hanging out of the window on the left side and the other G.I. was half in and half out of the door on the other side. Both were chewed up badly. We took a quick look around and made sure they were dead, then started out quick. As we started to pull away, I heard a man's voice from somewhere.

"Are you G.I.?"

After a few check questions to see if they were friendly, an Air Force Captain and an UNCACK female came out of the ditch where their wrecked Jeep was. They were coming back from Taegu and got caught in the guerrilla attack. He was smart enough to run his Jeep off the road into the darkness. To thank me, he offered me a ride in his A-26 attack bomber. The next day I went over to K-1 Airport. He had already gone up in the plane. I watched, and a few hours later they were back. I remembered 12 planes had gone up, but only seven came back. The next flight of 12 planes that went up, only six returned. One blew up just off the runway because an unexploded bomb hung up in the bomb rack. The biggest piece of the A-26 was a wheel that bounced 50 feet high off the runway. The Captain asked me if I was ready for a flight

"No thanks," I told him. "I'm going back to the ground war where it's safer."

Anyhow!

The problem was low flight attacks and lots of enemy ground fire. So I didn't get my ride over enemy territory.

Anyhow!

Brutality

One of the things I could not understand, then or now, was the brutality the Chinese and North Korean armies would impose on the women, children and the elderly in Korea – the kids especially. They were starved and tortured beyond belief. When we passed them, they looked upon us as if we were another army that was going to hurt them. The very food we soldiers disliked, they fought over like starved dogs. In their eyes, we were just another army that would hurt and kill them. Yet, when they got to know us, we couldn't get rid of them.

Most of them were children without parents. They accused us of murdering their parents. Yet when you talked to them – through an interpreter – the death of their parents came at the hands of an airplane with a red ball painted on it. We learned they were referring to when the Japanese attacked them in the 1930's. It was very difficult explaining to them it was not the United States, as we were not there at that time. The interpreters had it all wrong.

I had one little boy who had no coat or warm clothes. He shook like a leaf in the cold rain. I picked him up and held him close to feel my body heat. He finally stopped shaking. I gave him a fatigue jacket before I left. I've often wondered what happened to him. He tried to follow me, but couldn't keep up.

May God help us in this crazy world of wars and fights.

Anyhow!

Kid and Grenade

Often times moving through the valleys and rice fields, we passed through small villages lined with grass hutches or homes. When going through them we were warned to be aware of any questionable movements by the inhabitants. Normally, the people paid little attention to us, but stayed their distance, whether they were North Korean or South Korean.

This particular hutch seemed vacant. When we were passing through, this little kid, possibly 7 years old, came running out of the hut yelling at us.

"G.I.! G.I.! You my friend! You my friend!"

One of the sergeants put down a line of bullets right in front of him. The little kid skidded to a stop in the soft dirt.

"Hit the dirt!" The sergeant shouted.

We did, just as the hand grenade tied to the boy's back exploded, cutting the boy in half. All of us started firing on the shack he came from. We pretty much shredded the shack. Inside, we found a mother, two young girls, and a North Korean Guerrilla – all dead. To this day, I ask myself, *"Why do these things have to happen?"*

The treaty talks started February 1, 1951, and continued to early summer of 1953. All that time, there were a lot of wasted lives.

Anyhow!

Hill 1109

Before we went up the hill a second time, we were taking a short break. Next to us was a company of Turks. I often think this was very close to a third world war, considering the number of nations that fought in it. Sitting close to me was a Turkish non-com. I noticed his U.S. made M-1 sitting in the mud while he was sharpening his knife. I couldn't resist walking over to him.

"Don't you think you should be cleaning your rifle instead of sharpening your knife?" I asked him.

He didn't answer.

So, thinking he hadn't heard me, or didn't understand what I said, I asked him again, this time pointing at the rifle in the mud.

He grunted something about a sharp knife was better.

"Oh, well," I muttered and turned to leave.

"Hey! G.I.! Come back!" He said.

I turned back to him, surprised at his good English. He told me to sit by him, and he would tell me why a sharp knife was better.

He said when they go out on patrol, they come across Chinese outposts everywhere – and they *were* everywhere, usually with two soldiers. The Turks would stay close and wait for nightfall. Eventually, one of the Chinese guards would disappear into a small tent while the other one stayed awake on guard outside. The Turks would quietly sneak up and cut the guard's throat. Then, they would de-bone him like a deer and pile the meat and bones next to the Chinese guy sleeping in the tent. After carefully positioning the eyeballs on top, they would silently leave, not bothering the guy sleeping. The Turks figured that guy wouldn't sleep again for a long time.

The Turk told me some of the other horror war stories, but I told him to keep sharpening his knife. I left him thinking that whatever war I was ever in, I wanted the Turks on my side. I never saw him again. His outfit hit Hill 1109 on the East Flank; we hit it on the West Flank. The Republic Of Korea (R.O.K.) Company went straight up. It didn't matter how you attacked, there would be lots of wounded and dead.

Anyhow, like a crowded ant hill, Hill 1109 was thick with Chinese. I could never figure out how quick they could establish themselves between our ordered retreats before our orders to take it again. They were good at it. Every hole, depression or bush had a Chinese soldier in them. Their bullets were just as good at killing as ours were. Always, in the back of your mind was, *when is it my turn to die?*

I did get a leg wound on Hill 1109, so I was sent off to a MASH unit. They patched me up, and I was back in the war in a week.

We were at Hamhung and ordered back to cover the retreat of the 1st Marine Division from the Chosin Reservoir Hungnam area. There were ships in the Tonham Bay. I sometimes think General MacArthur had the right idea – "Keep right on going through China and into Russia." But then I think of some of the consequences.

The 24th Division covered the northeast flank of the retreat. The harbor below us was loaded with ships. The Iowa and Missouri were circling the inner harbor. First one, then the other. The Missouri was the first, then the Iowa.

Anyhow!

They would fire two salvo's of their 16-inch guns, and then
they would have to re-circle and correct the fire again. If you
were quick, you could watch the ring of smoke from the
nine 16-inch guns out over the valley. After awhile, you
could see the shells heading up the valley. They looked like
Volkswagen bugs flying through the air. After several
seconds later, you could hear the *whump, whump* of the
shells going off some 25 miles up the valley. You could see
the Chinese troops about a mile behind the Marines. I found
a 30 caliber machine gun and started firing at the Chinese. I
caused a small war all by myself. Before long, other machine
guns, the quad 50's and the 105mm were all firing randomly
at the Chinese. It slowed them down.

Anyhow, along with the Marines came thousands of
refugees getting away from the Chinese. They loaded every
ship possible, then burned the harbor facilities. I remember
getting wounded in the shoulder. Then a helicopter took me
back to the MASH Unit. A week and a half later, I was back
in the war.

One time somewhere near Wonsan, the main body of the
24th Division was catching hell from a Chinese artillery
company a few miles away. It was a day of lousy weather in
the high 20's and a mix of snow and rain. Strong winds
from the north kept our aircraft from flying. So, our
company – roughly 250 G.I.'s – put two platoons together –
100 G.I.'s – at the base of the hill about midnight, and we
started up a small ravine that would put us higher at the
rear of where they had the big guns and mortars. My right
foot was numb from the wet and cold. I had a difficult time
walking and staying quiet. We arrived at the top after
quietly killing two of their rear guard outposts – two
Chinese at each post. We aligned ourselves ready to charge
down into the slight depression where they were. They were
not expecting us to come in behind them. After we had time

to align ourselves, the flares were shot off, lighting the area up like high noon. My platoon lost 4 men and a few were wounded. I don't know what the casualty and wounded was for the other platoon, but I know they lost some.

For the Chinese, it was a slaughter. We were ordered to take no prisoners due to our situation. Out of their 200 men, none were left alive.

We spiked (drove a barbed steel spike into the touch-hole making the gun unusable) the big guns and damaged the mortars beyond repair. When we were ready to leave, we put a time fuse in their ammo tent and hurriedly left. I didn't sleep well the next few nights.

Vehicle Recovery Team

Every so often, usually every six months in combat, you would get to go on R&R – Rest & Recuperation.

On my second R&R, I asked my C.O. if I could have it at the same place as before, the motor pool in Pusan. All of Korea was a combat zone; there was nowhere you could call safe. You never knew where the Guerrillas would attack or a farmer would shake your hand and possibly stick a knife in you. My staying in Korea counted as combat time.

The motor pool was where I had friends and a lot of freedom. One day a Corporal came to me and asked if I knew about carburetors. Thinking he needed some special work, I gladly told him I had a long history of carburetor repair. Five G.I.'s would go out into the open and recover a Jeep, or a 2½-ton truck, a tank or whatever. The soldiers included: an ignition troubleshooter; a carburetor man; someone who knew wheel repair and body work, and a *booby trap* specialist.

The booby trap G.I. went first to check for any booby traps on the vehicle. Then, the other four would check their respective areas of expertise. If the vehicle would start and run, it would be recovered back for total repairs.

Now, you talk about being dumb! We risked five men for an expendable vehicle.

Anyhow, when we left our camp, we made sure there was no moon – nearly pitch black – and a very quiet night. Even then, there was a good chance the Chinese had the vehicle targeted in with mortar fire. We were out there working; the booby trap man was on guard for us; and I don't know how it got to us, but a tank retriever came upon us. I had the carburetor off and was preparing to install a rebuilt one on a Jeep. Then we heard a booming voice.

"You fellers need any help?"

These tank retrievers are big – really big – but very quiet. The operator sits about 12 feet off the ground. They're built to straddle a small tank, pick it up like in a sling of lumber, and haul it off. When that voice cut through the air, I thought God was asking if I needed help. I about crapped my pants. Everything was okay though, and the tank retriever picked up the Jeep and hauled it away, even though it was out there to retrieve a tank. It left, and we went on to another vehicle. I lasted one night and was ready to go back to the front lines of combat.

When I was back and on R&R, the guerrillas attacked the UNCACK compound. I was stationed right next to the compound. The guerrillas had already infiltrated the compound. The people inside were civilians and high-ranking officers. Four of us crept out into the dark night and slipped quietly inside the compound. All of the guards had been killed. We split up, and I ended up in the galley. I heard whispering in English.

In a loud whisper I said, "I'm a G.I.! Don't shoot!"

It was a bunch of high-ranking officers; one was a 3-star general. About seven or eight civilian American women were also in there. I explained we better get out of there, because I had no knowledge of how many Chinese were there. Right at that time, two Chinese soldiers came through the door. I had my carbine on full automatic, so I shot both of them. Then, I pushed the officers and women out the back door, and I told them to head for the G.I. motor pool compound. I shot four more Chinese guerrillas, but I didn't know for certain who they were in the darkness. They hadn't identified themselves.

When we were safe, the 3-star general thanked me and asked my name and what outfit I was with. I thanked him, but the best part was getting hugs and kisses from a real stateside woman. That was unheard of in Korea. The next day, I went over to see who I shot. They had already hauled the bodies away.

If someone were to ask me about my dislikes of war, I would have to say all of it. The smell of nitrate from the shells. The smell of rotten and burned flesh from the dead bodies. The torture of the captured G.I.'s. The torture their own people endured because of the communist beliefs, and my list could go on forever.

One night, I was really hot, and we knew an attack was coming. All night long the enemy sounded bugles, beat on pans, and yelled and screamed. I guess they were after the *After Life*. We were ready to give them their wish. Where I was, there were two battalions, hundreds of quad 50's, 105mm and 155mm artillery and many G.I.'s with machine guns and M-1 rifles.

Just prior to daybreak, it started. There must have been thousands of Chinese strung from one hill to the next and 8-10 deep. A few had rifles, others had bugles, and some were beating pans. All of them were screaming. We shot our flares continuously to light up the area. Seeing it sent chills up your spine. When they got within 500 yards, our side started shooting. One 50 caliber bullet can go through three Chinese soldiers. That, along with the other weapons, made it a slaughter. After two or three days in that heat, the smell was horrible. When daylight came, the Air Force dropped napalm.

After 60 years since the signed treaty, I can still see that picture.

Anyhow!

War is a bad experience, although it happens, and we have to live with it. I think if there were only two people on earth, they would have differences that would lead to arguments and eventually fights. And sooner or later, war.

God help us.

My friend, Shorty

Shorty Gaggan was more clever and sneaky than he was smart. Oh, don't get me wrong, my buddy Shorty was smart, too, really smart, but he had a weakness – beer.

You see, beer was plentiful in Korea. If you knew the system, age was not an issue, and Shorty knew how to play the system.

When our platoon moved north across the 38th parallel, we came upon an abandoned bunker. We never did figure out who it belonged to, but it was ours now. The base was deep, probably dug out by a big Cat. The sides were made up of old railroad ties, and the ceiling was put together with braced railroad ties. It was approximately 20 feet wide and 40 feet long. Then, it was covered by really deep camouflage. It looked like a good place to hold up for a spell.

The best thing about this bunker was an old pot-bellied stove in the middle. Now, mind you, it was late winter in 1952, and really cold and wet. It didn't take me and the other guys long to scrounge up some wood from the surrounding trees. We stoked up that old pot-belly until it glowed hot. We were so comfortable that our platoon lieutenant decided to stay for awhile. Make no mistake, that old stove was puffing up something fierce, and no doubt was putting a line of smoke into the sky above. We decided we would just take our chances.

At one end of the bunker, we found a stash of old bunks, the G.I. fold-up type. We posted guards all around our perimeter, and the rest of us set up bunks and turned in. We had set up a regular schedule of relief for the posted guards.

Anyhow, Shorty found himself some beer − a lot of beer − somewhere in the middle of the night. We never did find out where he got beer, but he always seemed to manage it. That night, he came back to the bunker really drunk. He had a tough time recalling our secret password, but he managed. He staggered in and warmed up a cup of coffee on that old stove. Poor old Shorty needed a spoon to stir his sugar and creamer, but he couldn't find his own. Over my bunk was a long chunk of wood with nails, which everyone used to hang their cups and utensils. Shorty came innocently over to my bunk to borrow mine, since he couldn't find his. In doing so, he rattled the utensils in my cup. Might as well have been London's Big Ben chiming off at midnight.

After a time in combat, every soldier develops a kind of sixth sense regarding nearby danger. Those rattling utensils elevated my senses to a new high. My reaction was instant. I grabbed Shorty by his crotch and his shirt and literally threw him over my bunk and the one next to me. Shorty landed on the next one over that one and crashed down on George Satawa. George's senses went off like mine did, and like lightning, George was pounding my friend into a bloody mess. It was all we could do to stop him.

"All I want is a cup of coffee," Shorty kept repeating.

"Ya could a got yourself killed!" I yelled.

"Over a damn cup of coffee!" George said. "You drunk again, Shorty?"

"Yeah, I think so."

"We know so," I said. "Where did you get the beer?"

"Not sure," Shorty slurred.

"Well, beer or no beer, you better start remembering the passwords," George said. I don't think George really cared. Shorty bled for a full day after the beating. When our lieutenant asked what had happened to Shorty, we told him Shorty fell down a ravine when he went out to pee during the night.

A few nights later, beer-slurping Shorty did it again – too much beer. He wandered back to the platoon, but this time he was so soused he couldn't remember the password. He slurred words and numbers and stumbled around in circles. The guards had their instructions. They shined lights on him, but no one recognized him. They asked him three times for the password, but Shorty couldn't remember it.

Friendly fire happens in every war, and Korea was no exception. And there are lots of stories about the effect of a . 50 caliber bullet on the human body. When our guards put two .50 caliber bullets through Shorty's lower body, all that held him together was his backbone and a few strands of meat and tendons.

Instant death!

That's war.

I cried that time. Shorty was my good friend.

Anyhow!

Anyhow!

Korean Train Troop

The rail system in Korea was very narrow in width. After my first R&R, they put us on a train to be taken from Pusan to Pyongyang, where I was with my old 24th Division. On the way, we were attacked by guerrillas. Thank God the biggest caliber they had was a 30mm cannon. A few G.I.'s got wounded, and there were lots of holes in the train, not to mention a lot of broken glass. What sent chills down my back was laying there on the floor of the train car and looking up to see where that beautiful female voice was coming from singing, *God Bless America*. It was movie star, Yvette Mimieux. She was standing up singing and walking back and forth stepping over us. Now that takes guts. She has been my favorite star ever since – female star, that is. All of us sang with her, but we laid flat on the floor while doing it. She was great. Usually, the female stars stuck to the officers. The lowly G.I.'s have to sit back and watch.

Anyhow!

My Last Fight

It was a very cold night the first part of November, 1952. My Company D of the 24th Division was waiting for dawn at the southerly border of Pork Chop Hill. We were about to take the hill for the fifth time. The Chinese held it at that time.

The whistle blew and we proceeded to advance up the hill. A million things were flashing through my mind.

Is it my turn?

Am I going home without arms or legs?

When is this *game* going to end?

Am I going to see Christmas?

As cold as it is, why am I sweating?

Why am I so tired?

Maybe if I put my M-1 down, I could move better – dumb! Or maybe I drop my field pack – really dumb.

There was no fire from the Chinese as yet. But then we were still only a short distance up the hill. Oh, why didn't I get some sleep last night? Soon, the numbness was finally gone from my right foot ad I could move much easier. *Zip!* A bullet sped past my ear. Will I hear the one that hits me? Will I die on this trip of the hill? *Zip!* Another round so close I could feel the heat. Then another fire fight started nearby. *A G.I. flame thrower*, I thought – *burn them all!*

Zip!

Zip!

Return fire was increasing and I hadn't even fired my own M-1. Climbing the hill really caused sweating. Climb, climb, climb. Crawl, crawl, crawl. Every time a flare went off, it was crawl, get shot, or lay still.

Zip!

Anyhow!

Oh, God! When will this end?

Just ahead of me was a hole in the mountain. What do I do? I threw a live grenade inside and kept moving. I was nearly to the top when I noticed my left pant leg was all bloody, and my boot was filled with blood. It was then that I realized a bullet had grazed the left side of my belly and torn my shirt. I was bleeding profusely. I yelled for a medic who arrived shortly. He put a butterfly bandage on my wound and then wrapped it tight with another bandage. He abruptly started to leave me.

"Hey!" I yelled.

"What?"

"How about a copter ride to a MASH unit?"

The medic grunted something inaudible and kept marching away. He took a few more steps then came back. "Tell you what, Soldier. You go up there and tell that Chinese feller who shot you to do it again. But this time put the round a couple of inches to the left. Then I'll come back with a shovel and wheelbarrow and I'll personally haul you up to the MASH unit."

Combat humor at its finest.

Anyhow, I continued to the top of Pork Chop Hill once again. I rejoined the rest of my platoon. Out of 52 soldiers we lost 7 with many wounded. We immediately dug in for the inevitable counter attack. It came almost immediately, but it was weak and unorganized. We repelled it with few casualties.

We dug in waiting for the next counterattack. All night long they blew bugles, beat on pans and babbled over loud speakers. The attack came and it sent chills down your spine. We were outnumbered ten to one, but we held. We knew it was coming again. We sent out men to find what was left of the company. We found a total of nine G.I.'s, including us. Included in that count was a full-bird colonel and he was badly wounded. He started to get on the radio and ask for permission to retreat. I did so, but someone said to *stand by.*

"How long?" I asked. My gosh, we were facing a serious threat of being wiped out. I reminded them there were only nine of us and three or four were wounded. Again, we were told to *stand by.*

"Son," the colonel said.

"Yes, Sir," I said, but it kind of irked me being called son.

"Can you get us off this hill?" He asked me.

"Yes, Sir, I'll do anything to get us off this hill."

He struggled to sit up some, then stared me straight in the face. "Give them ten minutes, then get us down this hill. You are now a battle commissioned second lieutenant."

"Sir," I said with a hard swallow, "I'm only a Pfc, but if it gets us off this hill, I'll do it."

Ten minutes later we started down the hill with the Chinese right on our butts. One of the wounded soldiers died on the way down. I turned the colonel and the wounded over to two United Nations medics. I believe they were Scottish. The other six of us went to the nearest headquarters to be interrogated. They gave me my orders to return to the replacement depot at Pusan. I was on my way home.

After a week at the replacement depot worrying about being recalled back into combat, I was on the USS Collins coming home. The trip home was a nightmare because of the overload. Meals were sparse – only 2 a day. Barrels of oranges were out on the deck for in between the two meals. A few hundred G.I.'s slept on deck in turns, which reminds me of an amazing event just days after we left for home.

My UFO Sighting

About three days out of Osaka, Japan, we were heading for San Francisco. Because the USS Collins Victory ship, a troop transport, was overloaded with 5,500 G.I.'s, approximately one third of us rotated sleeping on the deck.

My first turn sleeping on the deck was quite an adventure. That particular night seemed darker than usual. I was sitting up against a bulkhead, half asleep, half awake, but my eyes were closed. A light on my eyelids caused me to respond with a mumbled, *Yes, Sir!* thinking it was the officer of the deck. He didn't answer, so I opened my eyes to find no one was there. But what *was* there was a round, green and white ball, rapidly approaching from the rear of the ship before stopping off the starboard side.

It stopped on a dime!

Anyhow!

It hovered there for a few minutes like it was watching us, then it zipped off to the right over the horizon in a matter of a split second.

The next day, the ship's captain came on the loud speakers and answered everyone's questions.

They didn't know what it was, but it definitely was a UFO.

It could stop on a dime from an extremely high speed.

Estimated elevation was 1,000 feet.

It hovered off the starboard side of the USS Collins for one half to a full minute.

It left at 90 degrees from the approach path and disappeared over the horizon in a matter of a split second.

Estimated speed: 30,000 miles per hour.

End of Event

It took 18 days to get to the Golden Gate Bridge. When our ship was twenty to twenty-five miles out. We saw the north tower of the bridge as it came into view. The noise we made could have been heard in San Francisco. Oh, what a beautiful sight. When we went under the bridge, over 100 whores were hanging off the sides above us, each one holding a sign with her phone number on it. All of them wore short skirts with no panties on. For a lonely G.I. who spent 1 ½ years in Korea, it was like taking a whole bottle of vitamin pills.

We arrived at the dock in Oakland and unloaded. A line fifteen deep of goofy G.I.'s went on forever. It was kind of like looking down a railroad track. It kind of comes together a long distance away. We were sent to Camp Stoneman where they prepared us for the rail travel to Colorado City, Colorado.

Anyhow, on the dock we got a golf ball/orange attack from the people over the fence. And after 1 ½ years of fighting for their freedom left us with pretty bad feeling. They gave us passes each day until the next troop train took off. Four of us immediately went to the nearest restaurant and ordered two gallons of milk and three platters full of sliced tomatoes heaped 6" high. In Korea we only had powdered milk and no tomatoes. Their tomatoes had big white grub worms in them.

Anyhow!

Worse, they fertilized their tomatoes with human crap. Geez!

And you talk about royalty! Eleven – count 'em – eleven cars of antsy G.I.'s getting treated like kings. Thick, juicy steaks, eggs, real potatoes, tomatoes, and more and more. Even the Rock Island rocket pulled over to the side of the road to let us zip past.

We got on a troop train and headed for Colorado City, Colorado. In Ogden, Utah, they serviced the train for a half hour. I asked permission to get off and call my sister, Thelma, in Provo, Utah. It took three officers and one M.P. To allow me off the train with the same stipulation to return. The top officer agreed to let me call my sister. However, he ordered the M.P. To stand with his hand on the receiver to jerk it away if I didn't comply with their orders.

I told Thelma to go to the train depot in Provo. She, Carl, Penny and Pat came down to the depot. They couldn't tell Thelma anything, saying the train and the soldiers were all classified. So, they started to leave the depot when they were called to stop.

"You know," he said, "there is some real good scenery north, at the end of the loading ramp. You guys could probably take 15 or 20 minutes to see all of it."

My kin got the hint and we got to see one another at 60 miles per hour. It was all I could do to stay on the train instead of jumping off.

At Colorado City we went building to building in 20 degree weather in shorts, t-shirts and boots – we must a looked a little weird. They checked us for diseases, bad teeth, and just about everything else imaginable. At the end, there was a row of lieutenants that gave us our "214" service records. They read off what we had done and what medals we were going to get. This one lieutenant looked me up and down.

"Do you agree with what I just read to you, Soldier?"

"Well, Sir, I don't want to be facetious, but you have on this piece of paper that I got the Silver Star for some reason. Sir, I got wounded three times, yet there's no Purple Heart on this list. Heck, you don;t even have a Good Conduct Medal here. How do you explain that?"

"Soldier," he chuckled, "in the Army, we call that a *SNAFU*."

Anyhow!

It took me two years to find out what that meant: Situation Normal! All Fucked Up. Anyhow, I moved on and got me a fresh uniform, $300 and an Honorable Discharge."

I immediately headed for Lael in Yuma, Arizona to surprise her. Instead, I got the surprise when I found her in bed with another guy. I promptly turned around and headed for Mason City. She didn't even know I was there.

After getting out of the Army and the active reserves, I completed college at Iowa State College in Ames, Iowa. I got a job white-washing stucco houses and I met Marlene Moon and married her. We both lived at Pammel Court while I finished college. I graduated in June, 1955 with a BS degree in Forestry with year in a specialty of Wood Technology. I was offered a job in Washington D.C., but that was too far to travel. Then I was offered a job in Arizona, but too dang hot for me.

Then I got an offer with the Division of Forestry in Washington State. I elected Washington State because of the hunting and fishing opportunities and much better climate. Boy, was I ever out of my noggin!

We left Iowa with son, Mark, for Washington State. Our first home was in Burlington, Washington. Soon after, we moved to Mount Vernon, Washington. In 1957 we finally settled in Sedro-Woolley, Washington. In that time, we had two daughters, Amy and Cindy. We lived together for 9 years until I discovered Marlene couldn't stand me. So, after we divorced, I quit work at the Department of Natural Resources and went to work at Willis, Rogers, and Pearson Lumber Company as a timber buyer.

While buying timber in Bellingham, Washington, I met Denise. She was working at Howard's Cafe in Bellingham. It was odd, how we met. I was a day away from going on a 30-day vacation back to Waukegan, Illinois. I was in Howard's Cafe having lunch with four other timber sales buyers. I paid for all four meals. Denise was waiting on us. I gave my usual tip and left the next day on my trip. A month later when I returned, I went to the Forest Service Sale with another log buyer. We went to Howard's Cafe for lunch and had no sooner sat down than Denise came right over and dropped a dollar bill on the table right in front of me.

Anyhow!

"That's yours," she said.

"Whoa!" I said, very surprised and confused. "I've been gone for four weeks and haven't been in here all that time. You have to be mistaken."

"Nope," she grinned. "You and three others came in together for lunch. You all had a crab Louis. You paid for all four and gave me a $5 tip." Then, she walked off.

I wasn't born yesterday. I gave her a $5 tip and gave her the dollar bill back along with a note that said: *I will see you again.* I left it on the counter. Needless to say, I saw her again. We were married four months later.

I never have been with a woman like Denise. She was kind, considerate, thoughtful and a dang good wife and mother. She had two daughters and a son. Heck, I had two daughters and a son. Later, I legally adopted her son, Dennis. So, we had hers, mine and ours. How about that? We also had 30 years together of pasting those kids together. I had four jobs while she was a stay-at-home mother.

She definitely had the tougher job.

In 1986, we learned that Denise had cancer. She was treated with chemo and got another 10 years of life. They were tough and rough years, but in the end, me and Denise became very close.

After Denise died in 1996, I had a pretty dismal life. I guess I didn't show it, but my life seemed to have a hole in it. I started going to church, but the ladies made me feel like the feed thrown out to the chickens. I had already made up my mind not to marry again. Heck, where would I ever find another woman like Denise. And to this day, I still feel that way. I've dated many times since 1996 and had many opportunities to marry, but there was always something missing, so single I stayed.

Lonely, but happy.

After Denise died I did everything I could to stay busy, then get tired and go to sleep at night. I'd have some real bad dreams, mostly about my war experiences. Next morning, I'd get up and do it all again. Today, because of Peter Randolph Keim, I can talk freely about combat that happened almost 70 years ago. Well, maybe not all of it. Some of it will go to the grave with me. I just wish people could realize and fully understand and appreciate what a combat veteran goes through to give us the freedom we have. Oh, well!

I eventually joined the Elks Club, the Jr. Chamber of Commerce and renewed my American Legion membership. I joined the Wildcat Steelhead Club, the Chamber of Commerce and many other local organizations. Heck, I even joined the American Legion's Drum and Bugle Corp. I ran for Skagit County Commissioner and lost – thank God! I was never meant to be a politician.

As I write, I'd be remiss if I didn't back up a bit and say a few things about my family.

Kids' History

Debbie: by law, my stepdaughter – by mind and heart, my daughter.

The one thing negative/positive about Debbie was how naive she was – just about everything! Whether it was a joke, life in general, etc, not a clue.

Often, after a joke was told and everyone had laughed, she would finally laugh, but later she would go to someone and ask them to explain the punch line.

Yep! Looking back, I would have to say she was naive – very naive!

However, there will never be a minute of doubt she is, and was, a very good person.

Debbie was second only to Denise (my wife, her mom) as a catalyst holding our family together. Thank you, Deb! You were the icon of the kids, and also of me.

Mark: my son from my first marriage to Marlene Moon.

I can definitely say, Mark was too smart, okay, intelligent, for his own good. At age five he was asking me questions that I had to lookup the answers before I could answer him. All through school he was way ahead of the teachers. He skipped the 5th grade because he knew too darn much. He ended high school with an ROTC scholarship at Washington State College. It included room and board. Poor Mark only lasted one quarter – he got bored.

He quit college and became involved in drug dealing. He was ousted from Seattle when he got caught. They told him to vacate or go to jail. About this same time, because he was trying to involve the other kids into taking drugs, I kicked him out of my home and told him to never come back. That might sound cruel, but I have 5 other kids to think about. As it was, some of the other kids did try his drugs, mostly pot.

It's been approximately 40 years since then and I've received his telephone calls and seen him two or three times. Each meeting he made it clear he wanted to come home. He did stay at Cindy's house, my youngest daughter. Today she tells me that was a disastrous mistake on her part. She couldn't get rid of him except to lock him out.

Mark had everything going for him except he wouldn't listen to other people's experiences. I haven't heard or seen him in over 20 years.

Amy: my eldest daughter with Marlene Moon.

Amy lives in Seattle. I get cards and calls from her every now and again. She's married to Jeff Graham. Amy has more or less attached herself to Jeff's parents rather than me. I don't blame her as they are geographically closer and therefore do more things together.

I love her dearly, but she is more distant to me than my other children. She always sends me neat cards. The last one for my birthday said: *you're really old*. Hard to argue with that, I fully agree. I turned 89 as of October 1st, 2018. She has no kids and is more or less a *business-type person*.

When my first wife and I divorced, I had a real difficult time in splitting up the kids. The final agreement after great consideration and concern on my part, I was to raise Mark and

Marlene to raise Amy and Cindy. My difficulty was Amy. When finally alone, I eventually gave in on Amy. She cried and thought she'd never see me again. Marlene and I had very lenient visitation rights. I still would have argued more, but Cindy needed Amy – someone to grow up with. I was wrong, but that was it.

Amy was a very bright and understanding child. However, reality won over want. I don't believe that Amy ever realized in that final decision that it was as bad as some I made in Korea.

No matter, I still love her dearly.

Verna (Sheen): one heckuva strong-minded woman

Repeat, a *very* strong-minded person. For the amount of hoops and hurdles she went through in life, I truly admire and love her. Especially as I was one of her hurdles. However, at times I was her best friend. Understand, this is my perspective. She probably would not agree with me.

One hardship she went through was the loss of affection from her blood father. Richard, her biological father, always showed far greater love and affection toward Debby, Verna's sister, than to her. Many people could not see this, but Denise, Verna's mother, and I, her stepfather, often talked about it. I finally went to Richard and told him to share his affection or don't show up. In the meantime, I tried to be a close friend to Sheen (my nickname for Verna).

Many times I would give into her on decisions. It was like making friends out of two very stubborn people. Personally, I think we did the best we could.

At present, Verna has some health problems, but she'll probably out live me. Guess that's not saying much as I'm 89 years old. My heart and mind are with you, Sheen.

Anyhow!

Cindy: my turn around daughter

In her early teens, Cindy led a rather sordid lifestyle. She was with her mother, so I knew little about her.

First, there was the truck driver. His wife from New Jersey threatened me with having Cindy either leave her husband alone, or she was going to hurt my daughter. There was more, but Cindy changed shortly after the threat. Thank God for the better. I sincerely felt I was partly at fault as she felt I abandoned her in life and was lacking in affection. Especially when I remarried to Denise.

Things changed with her attitude and by the time when Denise was seriously sick with cancer, Cindy became an adult person mentally. She really helped mentally during the last days of Denise's life. Cindy became a very close friend along with being my daughter. She visited me quite often from her home in Maple Falls.

She comes around here every 4th of July and watches the parade with me. I'm very proud of her during the death of her husband in the form of a logging accident.

I'm looking forward to her next visit.

Dennis: now, here's one to draw to.

When Dennis was only five and we all were living in Mount Vernon, he had a tendency to run away from home.

One night, just before Christmas, we all made a batch of popcorn and were eating it while watching TV. Debbie would lay on the floor on her belly and Dennis would lay on top of her. H was always afraid of scary things on TV and being close to her helped with the scary things.

One night before TV, Debby said. "Where's Dennis?"

We all started looking for him. I opened the front door and here he was walking away from the house looking like Tom Sawyer with a stick over his shoulder and a bag on the end of it. Denise started after him, but I stopped her.

"Let me handle this," I told her.

Anyhow!

"I took off at a run and caught up to him at the corner. I might add, it was cold and raining, almost snowing.

"Where you headed?" I asked him.

"I'm running away from home," Dennis answered.

"Any particular reason?"

Dennis didn't make eye contact – no answer. He just kept staring off into the distance from where we lived on a hill overlooking Mount Vernon. I looked long and hard where he was looking. Below us, the lights of town looked awful inviting.

"Let me explain the situation to you," I said. "Down there it looks warm and cozy, but where are you going to stay? Do you have food and money? Really, Dennis, it's a cold cruel world down there."

He shrugged.

"Now, have a look back there," I said, pointing out our house. "Up here there are people that love you, take care of you, and they even have hot popcorn you can eat. Heck, they even have a TV you can watch. We all, including me, want you back. Now, that's one choice."

Dennis shuffled his feet, then looked up at me as if he was asking what was the other choice.

"Down there it's damned ornery for anyone, especially a kid. No one to take care of you or pop your corn. Now, here's where you gotta make the choice. But, if you decide to go down the hill to Mount Vernon, I don't ever want you to come back. You'll be hurting your mom and all the other people who love you. I'm leaving now, but remember, it's your choice."

I walked away praying that God would help me getting him back home. When I walked into the house, everyone wanted to know what happened. I told them to get away from the window and start watching TV and act like nothing happened.

I watched Dennis through a sliver opening in the curtains, hoping I had done the right thing. He started back. I reminded everyone to act like nothing happened. He came in, put his stick away on his bed, and came out to crawl on top of Deb. After five minutes, I finally spoke.

"Who wants ice cream?" But under my breath I said, "Thank you God. I owe you."

72

Anyhow!

From that day until he was in junior high school, he was a good boy. Then his school friend swayed him a little which included a little *pot*. I think he's insecure even to this day, but he's married and straightened out considerably.

I can remember when I found out he was sneaking out of the basement window – he slept in the basement – and was going to the neighbor's and doing a lot of bad things which included smoking more pot. It was a fairly warm night the night I caught him. I went down to his bed and laid down on it. It was right below the window he used to get out. About midnight, I heard him crossing the gravel outside the window. He slide the window open and put his feet on my bare chest.

"Oh, shit!".Dennis hushed as if hoping to not wake me up.

"Busted!"

That's not all that happened to him, but it's all I want to share.

That's my family in a nutshell. So, where were we, oh, to continue, I've been involved in many projects. My favorites are American Legion, Wildcat Steelhead Club and municipal projects. Next are two that I am very proud of.

Flyovers of the Fourth of July Parade in Sedro-Woolley. I've gotten to know the people at the flight museum. They have become good friends on the 4th of July. They put three AT6's over the parade at noon. It is very well liked and very impressive. I asked for them to fly as low as possible and as loud as possible. We got all that and three passes when the main body of the parade in on Ferry Street.

The Wildcat Steelhead Club has sponsored a kid's fishing derby every year the first Saturday in May. Lots of prizes and big fish. Many co-sponsors with money, equipment, prizes and much more, join in the fun. In 2018, the city of Sedro-Woolley and the mayor, Julia Johnson, are constructing a park around the pond for additional events. The club is lucky to have a mayor-friend like Julia – it really helps the fishing derby. I am also trying to get the Heritage Flight Museum to have a flyover that same day.

Somewhere along the way, someone asked me why I jumped through all the hoops and hurdles to get the permit to dredge the pond and organize the volunteer labor and equipment for a one-day fishing event. Well, first of all, I had a brilliant co-chair and his wife and many others, all friends. Tommy Thompson and his wife, Gail, were the drivers for me. When they moved to Tonasket, Washington, I thought I was done for, however, Bob Nielson came to my aid.

Why do I do it?

Well, one rainy and cold day, a little girl, maybe 6 years old and covered in mud head to toe, approached me. She was shaking from the cold, but her shiny, bright teeth illuminated her big smile. She was holding a 5-pound rainbow trout. That big smile crossed ear to ear. That would warm anyone's heart as it did mine. I was hooked! I realized that I would do anything to dredge that mud hole out into a deeper pond. I rank the word *dredge* with the same experience as if I walked into a bank with BOMB printed all over me. We now have the road system complete, the dangerous trees removed, and we're waiting to dredge.

Anyhow, I would have to include the Loggerodeo in the events I promote and liked. For years they would dump a log painted red, white, and blue off the bridge at Marbelmount. We have three stopwatches timing it down the Skagit River to the Sedro-Woolley Bridge. They sold tickets prior and there were cash prizes. I miss that event.

Epilogue

Anyhow, I have a few final thoughts.

Today, our liberal-socialistic school system and the teachers who teach, do not even teach about the Korean War. They do not tell their students that over 36,500 military men did not come back. Nor do they mention the 100,000 who were wounded. They do not teach enough about the other wars and the millions of casualties that secured the freedoms they enjoy today. As one G.I. who fought in Korea, freedom doesn't come without a price tag. You have to fight for it, and many have to die for it. Many others lose arms and legs.

Instead, our glorious schools tell them we should not get involved. We should not interfere with the ways of other countries. They teach we are arrogant Americans imposing our democracy on others. But what about the alternatives: Nazism, Communism, Russia, China, North Korea, and more. If you remotely think you would have the same freedoms you enjoy today, may God help you.

I did not ask to go to Korea, and at the time I wondered, why? South Korea, Japan and Germany are some of our best allies and have pretty much followed our principles. The United States is not always right, and we do not always do the right thing, but we try, and we have the right to speak freely and disagree with things. Thanks to our Constitution and Bill of Rights and all that other stuff, we have that privilege. Many countries do not give those rights to their people.

Wars are not right. They are ugly, but they have to happen. Seems we always have one guy that gets in control and wants to control the world – Kaiser, Hitler, Mussolini, and others. Luckily, free people band together and put those tyrants down.

How do they do it? *War!*

Anyhow, as often as we try smart dialogue to bring about peace, inevitably one thing leads to another. An argument can lead to a fight. A fight can lead to something short of war. Then the serious stuff begins with more people, more tempers and more differences. God help us.

The following is a newspaper clipping from the December 17, 1951 issue of the Coos Bay Times

'Night Before - - -' Korea, 1951

WITH U.S. 9th CORPS, Korea, December 17. - (U.P.) - Lt Col. Darrell T. Rathbun of (4349 Eighth North) St. Petersburg, Florida, offered a G.I. version of "The Night Before Christmas" today.

Entitled "A Korean Christmas Carol," is was:

'Twas the night before Christmas, and all through the tent
Was an odor of fuel oil (the stovepipe was bent).
The shoepacs were hung by the stovepipe with care,
In hopes that they'd issue each man a new pair.

Anyhow!

The weary G.I.'s were sacked out in their beds,
And visions of sugar-babes dances through their heads
When up on the ridge line there arose such a clatter
(A Chinese machine gun had started to chatter).
I rushed to my rifle and threw back the bolt,
The rest of my tent-mates awoke with a jolt.
Outside we could hear our platoon Sergeant Kelley,
A hard little man with a little pot belly.
"Come Yancey, come Clancey, come Conners and Watson,
"Up Miller, up Shiller, up Baker and Dodson!"
We tumbled outside in a swirl of confusion,
So cold that each man could have used a transfusion.
"Get up on that hilltop and silence that Red,
"And don't you come back till you're sure that he's dead."
Then, putting his thumb up in front of his nose,
Sergeant Kelly took leave of his shivering Joes.
But we all heard him say in a voice soft and light:
"Merry Christmas to all – may you live through the night."

Freedom is not free.

In closing, I'd like to quote from a famed speech by Ronald Reagan in 1961. He was the 40th President of the United States.

Freedom is never more than one generation away from extinction. We didn't pass it on to our children in our bloodstream. The only way they can inherit the freedom we have known is we fight for it; protect it; defend it; and

Anyhow!

then hand it to them with the well-fought lessons of how, in their lifetime, they must do the same. And if you and I don't do this, then you and I may well spend our sunset years telling our children and our children's children what it once was like in America when men were free.

Made in the USA
Monee, IL
28 April 2023